Raised By a Narcissist:

That Woman aka My Mother

Serena Bennett

Trigger Warning
This book discusses themes of narcissistic abuse, emotional manipulation, trauma, and childhood neglect, which may be distressing for some readers. Please proceed with caution and seek support if needed.

Mental Health Disclaimer
This book is intended for storytelling and informational purposes only. It does not replace professional psychological, medical, or legal advice. If you are struggling with trauma or abuse, please reach out to a qualified professional for guidance.

Free Accompanying Journal
Receive a free journal designed to support your healing as you reflect on the themes within this memoir. It includes gentle prompts and space for personal insight.
📨 Email info@serenabennettofficial.com to join the mailing list and get your copy.

DISCLAIMER

This book is a personal memoir based on my experiences, memories, and perceptions. It reflects my truth as I lived and understood it. Some names, identifying details, locations, and events have been changed, altered, or combined to protect the privacy of individuals. Any similarities to actual persons, living or deceased, are purely coincidental.

This book is not intended to defame, malign, or cause harm to any individual, family, or organisation. The narrative is based on my personal recollections, and while I have made every effort to present events truthfully, memory is subjective, and others may recall events differently.

The content of this book is not meant to provide professional advice, nor should it be used as a substitute for psychological or legal guidance. The opinions expressed are solely my own.

By reading this book, the reader acknowledges that it is a personal account and not a statement of absolute fact. Any interpretations, conclusions, or assumptions drawn by the reader are their own.

CONTENTS

INTERLUDE:
THE MORNING CLARITY

PROLOGUE

Only through our own soul's journey can we hope to reach the hearts of others and inspire healing.

- Jack Kornfield

On the morning of 18 March 2024, at precisely 5:55 a.m., a restless night brought me clarity. Insomnia has a way of dredging up thoughts we would rather bury, and in that quiet, sleepless hour, I realised that perhaps the key to my healing lay in telling my story. For decades, I have carried the weight of trauma inflicted by that woman. My body, diagnosed with irritable bowel syndrome years ago, has borne the physical manifestations of this pain and internal rebellion against unhealed wounds. No medication has ever brought relief, but maybe... just maybe, confronting these truths will.

This book is my beginning. My healing journey starts here. It is not just a recounting of events but a reclaiming of my voice, a declaration that I will no longer be defined by her narrative. This is my story, raw and unfiltered, a testament to resilience and the pursuit of peace.

CHAPTER 1:

A MOTHER'S LOVE?

PROLOGUE

Some mothers are not meant to nurture; they are lessons in survival. And the greatest gift you can give yourself is the realisation that your worth is not tied to their ability-or inability-to love you. The journey to healing is not about fixing the past but creating a future that honours the strength you found within yourself.

- Sylvia Salow

Not everyone sees their mother the same way. Some call her Mum, Mummy, or Mother-the matriarch, revered and cherished, placed on a pedestal. But for me, it is different. Over twenty years ago, I made a decision that reshaped my view of the woman who brought me into this world. I stopped calling her my mother. Instead, I began referring to her as "that woman." Why? Because the bond that should have nurtured and protected me was shattered by her narcissism, leaving me with scars that shaped the very core of who I am.

I was a child beaten with a belt, never hugged, never kissed, never told I was loved. My accomplishments were invisible, overshadowed by her praise for others. Every conversation, no matter how it started, became about her needs, grievances, and life. My struggles and triumphs were mere footnotes in the grand narrative she constructed around herself.

She despised my husband without cause, only to befriend him after our divorce, basking in the collapse of my marriage with a twisted sense of gratification.

I rarely speak of her. To do so is to relive the pain, to remain trapped in moments I have fought to leave behind. But there are times when the subject of family arises, and I am faced with a choice: to lie and paint a picture of a loving, supportive mother or to tell the truth about my experience. I choose the latter, for pretending serves no one, least of all myself.

CHAPTER 2:
IN HER WAY, SHE TRIED

PROLOGUE

Carl Jung, a prominent Swiss psychiatrist, suggested that the unconscious mind is influenced by archetypes and personal experiences, shaping how individuals respond to their environment. In relationships, these unconscious patterns often surface, as the mind works to reconcile feelings of love, duty, and personal limitations.

- Carl Jung

Psychologists often say even the most fractured relationships carry flickers of effort-however flawed or misguided. That woman, with her towering narcissism and sharp edges, was an exception. I never saw any hints of her being the mother she should have been; in her eyes, she was.

When I think back to my early years, her presence is strangely fragmented. I cannot recall if she worked. My father's routine etched itself into my memory-the door creaking open as he came and went, his heavy steps on the stairs-but with her, there is only a void. What I do remember is that she did provide the fundamentals. It was not the nurturing love I yearned for, but there was a roof over my head, clothes on my back, and meals on the table.

My wardrobe was never a source of pride. The clothes came mostly from the local rag market, many of them second-hand or slightly flawed. I still remember one particular pair of tights. To describe them, imagine toilet paper: one leg was thick, like four-ply, while half of the other leg was thin, like two-ply. The embarrassment of wearing them still lingers.

In the 1980s, pink Farah trousers were all the rage. I never dared to ask for them. Deep down, I knew my request would be met with a sharp refusal or, worse, the hollow echo of disappointment. Later, I did have one prized possession-a pair of blue Hi-Tec trainers. I can still feel the giddy pride of walking alongside my best mate, Alice, who had a grey pair, and revelling in our shared triumph, however small.

The house we lived in was modest but warm, and I had a room of my own. It was not much, but it was mine. The walls held my secrets and dreams; the floor bore witness to the moments when I felt most safe. It was a sanctuary of sorts, though the safety was often undermined by the tension that permeated the rest of the house.

Meals were her domain-her one undeniable skill. Every dish came from scratch, a reflection of her Jamaican roots. Steak or roast lamb was out of reach, as we ate what she could afford: liver and onions, tripe with butter beans, sprats & corned beef, and rice. She had a way of making something out of nothing, a resilience I grudgingly admire even now. Her curry goat, rice and peas, stew peas and rice, ackee and saltfish were her masterpieces. Ackee was expensive, so she often substituted cabbage, yet somehow it still tasted amazing. There was something grounding in those meals.

Emotional Reflections

But food and shelter were not enough. Looking back, the emotional void of my childhood is stark and unyielding. There was an absence that no amount of warm meals could fill. Love, I learnt early, was something to be earned. I spent years trying to decode how to win hers. Was it through obedience? Success? Silence? I do not know if she ever intended to send that message, but it imprinted itself on me all the same.

I felt alone in a house that was never empty. Loneliness was my quiet companion, a dull ache that hummed in the background of my days.

In the absence of warmth, I built walls. I learnt to seek validation elsewhere-often in ways that left me more broken than before. My reflection in the mirror told me stories of unworthiness. I internalised the belief that love had to be fought for, never freely given. That belief shaped me, shaping how I moved through relationships and how I saw myself.

Lessons Learnt

Now, as an adult, I can see the lessons she unintentionally taught me. Love, I have learnt, is not a currency to be earned but a gift to be given freely and consistently. Grand gestures are hollow without the daily rhythm of care and connection. I have built a life that rejects the emotional starvation of my childhood. My home is one of warmth and safety, not just in bricks and mortar, but in the intangible threads of love that bind us.

I have sought relationships that offer stability, replacing chaos with calm, and found family beyond blood ties. My children and grandchildren know the unconditional love I once craved. They will never doubt their worth or wonder if they must perform to earn my affection.

Yet, I also know no single relationship can fill every void. Balance comes in recognising the beauty of friendship, the strength of romantic love, and the necessity of self-care. My scars remain, but they no longer define me. They are simply reminders of where I have been and what I have chosen to leave behind.

In her way, she tried. It is a truth that will always sit uneasily within me-neither enough to heal the wounds nor small enough to ignore. I survived, and I have since reclaimed my life.

CHAPTER 3:

WHERE LOVE SHOULD HAVE LIVED

PROLOGUE

John Bowlby, a pioneering psychologist in attachment theory, emphasised the significance of early childhood experiences in forming the foundation for emotional bonds throughout life. The absence or presence of love during formative years profoundly impacts how one perceives and seeks connection in adulthood.

- John Bowlby

I have said the word "home" countless times, but it has always felt hollow on my tongue-a term I used out of habit, not belief. What I lived in was not a home at all. It was a house-a structure of bricks and mortar that offered shelter but little else. There was no warmth within those walls, no essence of love. It was merely a place where I existed. I was not nurtured. I was not loved. I did not belong.

A true home should be a sanctuary - a refuge from the harshness of the outside world. But in that house, there was no refuge. Instead, it was where the harshness seeped into every corner, where unhappiness clung to the walls like mould. I often wondered what it would feel like to return to a place that offered comfort and love. But that was not my reality.

What was missing, I realise now, was love. Love should have been the lifeblood of that house, flowing through its halls and filling its rooms. Love should have been the invisible thread connecting its inhabitants, binding us together with kindness and affection. But there was none. No nurturing touch. No comforting words. No tender gestures. My heart ached for the kind of love I knew I deserved, the kind I saw in stories or glimpsed in other families. But it was never there.

The absence of love was not just an emptiness-it was a void that swallowed hope and silenced dreams. I needed love to feel like I mattered, to give me the strength to face the world. Instead, I learnt to keep my voice small and my presence smaller, hoping to avoid notice and the sting of rejection.

A home should encourage growth-of the body, the mind, and the spirit. It should be a space where dreams are shared and worries are voiced without fear. But in that house, my thoughts were dismissed, my feelings ignored, and my voice unheard. It left me questioning if I had any worth at all.

I needed a mother who could be my guide, my anchor in life's storms. Someone who could help me see my own potential and remind me that I was not alone. But my mother's presence was anything but comforting. Her words, when they came, carried the weight of disappointment and criticism. Encouragement was a language she did not speak. I came to understand that love was not something she could give, no matter how much I longed for it.

The air in the house was always heavy with tension. Even silence felt loud, filled with unspoken words and unresolved conflicts. Laughter was an anomaly-something I only heard on the television. It was as though joy had no place in our lives. I often escaped into daydreams, imagining a home where laughter was abundant and love was tangible. A place where I could breathe freely without the constant weight of sadness pressing on my chest.

Looking back now, I see that a home should have been the foundation on which my future was built. It should have been a place of love and encouragement, a safe space where I could grow into myself. Instead, my house became a classroom of survival. I learnt to fend for myself, to bury my emotions, and to hide my vulnerabilities. I built walls around my heart, hoping they would protect me. And in many ways, they did. But at what cost?

Emotional Reflections

The weight of those years still lingers. The cold silences, the sharp words, and the deep loneliness-they left scars that have not faded. Sometimes, I wonder how different I might have been if love had lived in that house. Would I have been braver? Kinder to myself? The what-ifs are endless, but they are a road I have learnt not to travel too often.

Despite the pain, I recognise that those experiences shaped me. They taught me resilience, though I wish the lesson had been gentler. They forced me to find strength within myself when none was offered from the outside. And while they left me with wounds, they also gave me the determination to heal.

Lessons Learnt

From the absence of love, I have learnt its value. Love should not be something earned or withheld. It should flow freely, creating warmth and safety. A home should be a place where love thrives, where support and kindness fill every corner.

I have made a vow to myself to create the home I never had. For myself, for my children, for my grandchildren, for anyone who steps into my life. I am determined to nurture, to love, to offer the sanctuary I so desperately needed. My house growing up may not have been a home, but I have the power to build one now. And in doing so, I can finally give myself the love I deserved all along.

CHAPTER 4:
FRAGMENTS OF LIGHT:
THE FEW GOOD CHILDHOOD MEMORIES

PROLOGUE

Sigmund Freud, the founder of psychoanalysis, proposed that the mind can push distressing or traumatic memories into the unconscious to protect an individual from overwhelming emotional pain. This is more than likely the reason I have limited memory of good things from my childhood. But amidst the shadows, there were glimmers of light-moments I cherish, even if only in fragments.

- Sigmund Freud

Sunday Traditions: Family, Music, and Memories- Most Sundays felt like a pilgrimage to my nan's house, a ritual steeped in routine but laced with a quiet magic. The car ride itself was part of the charm - my dad's reggae music transforming the small interior of his Hillman Hunter transformed into a moving concert. The thrum of the bass, my little voice blending with the lyrics and my occasional offbeat claps in the back seat, created a rhythm that felt like home, if only for a while.

When we arrived, I would steal a fleeting ten minutes with my nan. Her soft voice and warm smile were like rare gifts in a world where such tenderness was scarce. But my real joy lay at the bottom of the road, in my cousin's house. We ran wild with laughter and games, the hours slipping by unnoticed until dinner summoned us back. The meal at my nan's was chaotic in the best way-uncles, aunts, and cousins creating a symphony of voices. The kitchen brimmed with the aroma of dinner. It was crowded, loud, and lively. I loved it!

The drive back to our house at the end of the day held its own kind of magic. As the car hummed along the dark roads, I would let the gentle motion lull me into a half-sleep. Without fail, I woke the moment the car stopped-a strange instinct that marked the end of those precious Sundays. On the weeks we stayed in the house, my dad's old reggae records filled the house. I would sit cross-legged on the floor, the album covers spread around me, singing along to the printed lyrics. Bob Marley was my favourite back then. Now, his music stirs something more bittersweet in me-a mix of nostalgia and loss.

Friday Nights: Anticipation and Family Takeaways - Friday nights carried a different kind of joy; one built on anticipation. By the time my dad's car pulled into the driveway, I was practically buzzing. Even from the top floor of our maisonette, I could recognise the hum of his car's engine, a sound so familiar it felt like a language of its own. The moment the keys jingled in the lock, my brother and I would race to the door.

Payday meant takeaways-a rare treat that felt like luxury. Fish and chips or fragrant Chinese food (normally chow mein) that filled the kitchen with unfamiliar but welcome spices. The meal itself was secondary to the feeling it brought-a fleeting sense of celebration, of being cared for.

Bittersweet Saturdays: Freedom, Sports, and Soup- Saturdays were bittersweet. I remember how the sun felt, warmer than usual as the promise of freedom hung in the air, only for it to dissolve by midday. There was always that one part of the day that pulled me back-Grandstand. It wasn't just a TV show; it was a monument of time. A sports program on BBC1, it broadcast live action and reports from every corner of the world. Three and a half hours stretched on for, but in my child's mind, it felt like an eternity. The screen filled with running commentary, the chatter of sportscasters, and flashes of events from stadiums I would never see. My dad, hogging the TV, would sit there, engrossed, as the minutes ticked by in that slow, relentless way.

And then there was Saturday soup. Not just any soup, mind you. No, this one was pronounced Sa-ti-deh Soup,' with its deep, rich Jamaican heritage woven into its very essence. Pumpkin, yams, potatoes, carrots, boiled skinny dumplings-spinners, they were called-and the star of the show: mutton. Or, when the purse strings were extra tight, pig tails would stand in as a cheaper alternative. The smell alone would flood the house, and I would feel the nausea rise in me. I could not stomach it. The combination of the pungent scent and the lingering, unyielding presence of Grandstand was a clash that pushed me to my limits. Hell on earth, I thought.

If I was not grounded-which was a frequent punishment in those days-I would bolt from the house as early as I could, leaving behind the heavy air. I was a tomboy; I hung out with the boys and the other girls who had that same adventurous spark in them, the ones who did not mind getting their knees scraped or their clothes muddied. Whether we were clambering up the school field, scrambling through the woods, or skimming stones by the lake, I felt free. Each moment was an adventure. The world, in all its wildness, was there for the taking.

Emotional Reflections

Looking back at those fragments of light from my childhood, I feel a sense of warmth mixed with sadness. The memories of Sunday visits to my nan's, the excitement of Fridays, and the freedom of Saturdays stand in stark contrast to the darker moments that were left behind in the shadows. These glimpses of happiness, though few and far between, still bring a sense of nostalgia. They remind me that even in the absence of a perfect childhood, there were moments of connection, belonging, and maybe even a little love. It is bittersweet to realise how easily those moments could fade into the past, leaving behind only faint echoes of what once was.

Lessons Learnt

From these fragmented memories, I've learnt the value of cherishing the small moments. Life is not defined by grand events but by the everyday interactions that shape who we are. I've come to realise that even the imperfect moments-like the frustration of Grandstand and the monotony of Saturday soup-hold their own significance. They taught me patience and resilience. I also learnt the importance of creating better memories for my own family. Despite my own childhood challenges, I've strived to ensure my children have experiences full of love, connection, and joy-memories they could carry with them as they grew, not unlike the fragments of light that rarely shone through my past.

CHAPTER 5:

THE MOTHER I FOUND IN MY AUNT

PROLOGUE

Melanie Klein, a psychoanalyst known for her work on object relations theory, proposed that early relationships with primary caregivers form the basis for internalised representations of love and care. These internal objects can extend to other figures in a child's life, such as aunts, who may offer maternal warmth and guidance.

- Melanie Klein

The mother I should have had was my aunt Cynthia-the sister of that woman. If it was possible to choose your parents, I would have chosen her without hesitation. Aunt Cynthia, as we always called her, even as adults, out of respect and admiration, was an extraordinary woman.

Despite being in a committed relationship for over two decades, she never had children of her own. Whether this was by choice or fate, I will never know, but because of this, my brother and I became the centre of her maternal world. She treated us as though we were her own.

We were not spoilt, but we were given things and experiences that that woman who birthed us never provided. Money may have played a part, but it was also her maternal nature that made the difference. That woman lacked the instincts that Aunt Cynthia seemed to have in abundance.

I have countless cherished memories of my time with her. My love for Billy Connolly, the Scottish comedian, stems from her influence. She had a collection of his stand-up comedy videos, which I would watch eagerly whenever I visited. Looking back, I realise those videos were meant for adults, but I was too young to understand the mature themes.

Visits to her home were like stepping into a warm embrace. Unlike the strict rationing of treats at my house, Aunt

Cynthia's house offered an endless supply of things like orange and pineapple juice (which were classed as luxuries at my house), along with a selection of goodies. It felt like being on holiday at an all-inclusive resort.

Her bed was the epitome of comfort and indulgence. Even at ten years old, I had to climb onto it, and once there, I would sink into a plush duvet and pillows. It was heaven compared to the basic sheets and eiderdown I had at my house.

When Aunt Cynthia passed away after battling lung cancer, my world crumbled. Over a decade has passed but the loss still feels fresh. They say time is a healer, but some wounds remain. To add to the pain, that woman attempted to prevent me from attending her funeral, ordering my brother not to share the details with me. Thankfully, he ignored her wishes, enabling me to say goodbye to the closest thing I ever had to a mother.

Looking back, I see so much more clearly. When I in my mid-teens, I went on my first holiday abroad with that woman, my Aunt Cynthia, my uncle Lennox, and my brother. At the time, I thought that woman had taken us on that trip, but I now realise it must have been funded by my aunt and uncle. That woman could never have afforded such a holiday.

I miss Aunt Cynthia deeply. She was the closest thing to a mother that I ever had.

Emotional Reflections

The love I received from Aunt Cynthia shaped so much of who I am today. Her home was more than a place-it was a sanctuary. The comfort, acceptance, and joy she offered were things I never truly experienced elsewhere.

Losing her left a void that has never been filled, but her presence in my life taught me what it feels like to be loved unconditionally. Her kindness and warmth are etched into my soul. She gave me the motherly bond I craved until her time was unfairly cut short.

Lessons Learnt

Love is not limited by blood. Aunt Cynthia showed me that the bonds we choose can be stronger than those we are born into. Her willingness to give, not just material things but also her time and affection, left a lasting impact. Small acts of kindness can create lifelong memories and change someone's perspective. True family is defined by love, not by birthright.

CHAPTER 6:
MY BROTHER'S KEEPER:
A JOURNEY OF SIBLING BONDS

PROLOGUE

Erik Erikson, a developmental psychologist, highlighted the importance of sibling relationships in shaping personal identity and emotional development. Siblings often serve as companions and mirrors, helping each other navigate the challenges of growing up, providing mutual support and forming enduring emotional ties.

- Erik Erikson

Despite having several half-siblings on my father's side, I have only one full younger brother, Tyrone. The day he was brought back to our house from the hospital, I felt like everything changed. I was the only child up until then, and the limited affection and attention I was receiving would now be shared with this baby. I can still recall the discontent that swelled inside me. At that moment, I felt as if my world had come to a crashing halt. A new presence had arrived, a baby who demanded affection and attention that I longed for. It did not help that I could not fathom why my parents were so caught up with him. Tyrone's arrival turned my life upside down, and I could not help but resent him for it.

But as I grew older, something shifted inside me. I started to accept the title of big sister,' and with it came an understanding of my role. I was not just older in age but also in responsibility. I became Tyrone's protector. Like all siblings, we fought-over petty things, the trivial disagreements you experience as children. We would throw accusations back and forth, blaming each other for whatever went wrong. But there was one thing that was clear: I was the only one allowed to pick on him. No one else dared to hurt him without facing my wrath.

I remember one particular day, vivid as if it happened yesterday. Tyrone was playing out in the playground at the back of our maisonette, laughing with his friends. I heard a commotion from outside, and seconds later, Tyrone came running in, his face streaked with tears and a look of shock and pain in his eyes. Someone had hit him. Without hesitation, I slipped into my pumps, grabbed his toy cricket bat, and stormed out the door. The world around me blurred, and all I could focus on was the person who had dared to hurt him. My heart raced, and my anger burnt like fire. That moment-my instinct to defend him-was more than just sibling rivalry. It was the fierce bond we shared.

But then, everything changed. When Tyrone was nearly thirteen, he left our house to live with our dad. He had escaped. Tyrone was lucky-he avoided the hell that life at our house was, especially as a teenager. I was not so fortunate. I stayed, and the years that followed were a constant battle against the strictness of my upbringing. It was not long before I too reached my breaking point. At seventeen or eighteen, I finally walked away, though my relationship with that woman was still close, albeit from a distance.

As adults, Tyrone and I remain close, despite that woman attempting to drive a wedge between us. I made the choice to cut her from my life entirely, like excising a tumor. (More on this later on.) Tyrone, however, endures her toxicity. Even now, she treats him with disdain, using money as a bribing tool to manipulate him. I can see the toll it takes on him. I think he feels he needs her in a way that I never did. So, instead of cutting her off, he has chosen to manage his relationship with her by giving her space and time, letting her cool down before re-establishing contact.

Emotional Reflections

Reflecting on my relationship with Tyrone, I realise just how much it shaped me. At first, he was the reason for my frustration and resentment, as I felt that he took away the little shred of hope of being loved. But over time, he became my anchor. He was the one constant, the one person who knew the chaos of our house, and still, somehow, we clung to each other. He gave me purpose when everything around me felt uncertain. My role as his protector solidified our bond, and in return, I found a sense of meaning, a reason to endure.

It hurts to watch him still endure the weight of that woman and her toxic presence. I feel helpless as I see him navigate her outbursts, a journey I walked away from. But I understand that healing is not a one-size-fits-all process. His decision to stay in contact with her, despite everything, is his way of coping. It is a reminder to me that we all deal with pain differently. Some of us cut ties, and some of us try to mend them. Neither way is wrong; it is just what we can bear.

Lessons Learnt

The bond between siblings is powerful-one of the strongest forces I have ever known. It is a love that endures even when everything else seems to crumble. Protecting someone goes far beyond just standing up for them physically; it is about being there, emotionally, when life challenges them. Through the years, I have learnt that true protection means showing up not just in the good times but in the painful ones as well.

I have also realised the importance of boundaries for my own well-being. Walking away from toxic relationships was the right choice for me. It was not easy, and there are days when I wonder if I should have fought harder. But in the end, I had to protect my own peace. Tyrone's way of dealing with that woman has taught me to accept that healing does not look the same for everyone. Sometimes, it means staying connected, despite the pain. Sometimes, it means creating space to breathe before re-engaging.

Our shared experiences growing up gave me a resilience I never thought I would need. They taught me that strength is not just about surviving what life throws at you but about learning how to thrive despite it. It is about finding your footing, building meaningful connections, and understanding that survival is not the final destination-living fully is.

And perhaps most importantly, I have learnt to forgive myself. The decisions I made in the past-whether they were right or wrong-were the best I could do at the time. I have come to understand that we all do the best we can with the hand we are dealt. And that is enough.

CHAPTER 7:
UNDER HER RULES:
A JOURNEY THROUGH
RESTRICTION AND REBELLION

PROLOGUE

Virginia Woolf once wrote in A Room of One's Own that freedom is only another word for nothing left to lose. For those bound by strict rules, rebellion often becomes the only path to reclaim a sense of self.

- Virginia Woolf, A Room of One's Own

I grew up in a household where freedom was a foreign concept. Unlike my friends and even my cousin, who was just a year older, I was not allowed to go to discos, and I always had to be back in the house earlier than everyone else. It felt as though I was bound by invisible chains, anchored to rules that suffocated me. My life was a list of things I could not do. No boyfriends, no friends round to play or sleeping over -not that they wanted to. Even now, after decades have passed, three of my closest friends, who have been in my life since we were seven years old, admit they still feel intimidated by her presence. Even without speaking, she made them uneasy. Knocking on my door to call for me filled them with fear.

Punishment was a constant companion during those years. It was doled out based on what I had or had not done-grounding for smaller infractions, but worse for the more "serious ones. The phrase, "You were going to get this, but now you are not, was thrown around often, a sting I learnt to numb with a simple mantra: "You cannot miss what you never had. Severe punishment came in the form of beatings. She used her hand or a belt, the latter a weapon she wielded without hesitation. One time, she even struck me in the street, in front of my friends. That memory burns brightly in my mind-the humiliation of being beaten in public for daring to leave the house after she told me to get out of her house.

Clearly, her words were not meant to be taken literally. Where was child protection services when I needed them?

Our house was in a predominantly white neighbourhood, with only a handful of Black families nearby. Of those, she got on with maybe two. The rest were avoided, ignored, or dismissed over petty disagreements. One exception was Merlene, though their connection was tainted by suspicion. She believed Merlene was having an affair with my dad. Years later, her suspicions were confirmed. Merlene's son, Omari, confessed to me as an adult that his mother and my dad had indeed been involved. He also revealed something else: his relentless bullying of me at school was retaliation for how my dad had treated him and his brother. He believed his mother deserved better and took his anger out on me. Knowing this brought clarity but no comfort.

Unlike my friends, I was not allowed boyfriends, but I had them anyway, starting around the age of thirteen. One of them, Dan, was a couple of years older. He would throw stones up at my bedroom window from the adjacent garages late at night, and if the coast was clear-if she was asleep-he would sneak into the back garden. I would creep downstairs to see him, feeling like Juliet and Romeo, a forbidden romance. Those stolen moments of connection were a lifeline, fleeting but precious.

I remember one particular night vividly. I was about thirteen and had been allowed to attend a birthday party at a church hall. Dan came too, bringing alcohol. It was my first experience of getting drunk. I was terrified she would find out. Dan, equally petrified, did his best to sober me up before I crept back in the house. It was a moment of rebellion wrapped in anxiety, a bittersweet taste of the freedom I craved.

Any accomplishments I achieved were invisible, overshadowed by her praise for others. It was not overt criticism, but the comparisons stung. "They are better than you, her words seemed to imply. Every success felt diminished, unacknowledged. It was as if I was perpetually running a race I was never meant to win.

The most harrowing part of my adolescence, though, was something I buried deep for years. Around the age of ten or eleven, I was raped. The trauma of that day was compounded by the knowledge that I could not tell her. Fear of blame and punishment silenced me. I locked the memory away, refusing to confront it until I was in my mid-forties. It was then, while speaking with my childhood friend Loren, that I finally allowed the words to come out. Loren had been with me on the day it happened, and sharing the burden with her was both painful and freeing.

By my late teens, the suffocation of her rules became unbearable. At seventeen, having left school and started working, I was still expected to follow a strict curfew. Coming back to the house from work at six, I would go out with friends only to have to be back by nine. It was the final straw. I needed freedom, no matter the cost. At nearly eighteen, I declared myself homeless and moved into a bedsit, sharing accommodation with women who claimed to be "ex criminals. It was not ideal, but it was freedom-or so I thought. That freedom was short-lived, as within a year, I found myself trapped in an abusive relationship. When I discovered I was pregnant, that woman made her feelings brutally clear, calling me an embarrassment to the family and insisting I "get rid. When I refused, I had no choice but to swallow my pride and beg to move back into her house. I stayed just long enough to have my baby and secure a flat of my own.

Emotional Reflections

Reflecting on those years, I see a pattern of rebellion born from suffocation. If I had been given even a little freedom, perhaps I would not have sought it so recklessly. Drinking, skipping school, shoplifting, and early relationships were all acts of defiance against a life that felt unbearably constrained. I yearned for autonomy, for a sense of self that was not defined by her rules.

Her definition of love, if it was love, came with conditions and comparisons. I was measured against others and always found wanting. My accomplishments were dismissed, and my struggles were ignored. In many ways, I felt invisible, reduced to an extension of her will. It shaped me, leaving scars that I carry to this day.

Lessons Learnt

From those shadows of adolescence, I learnt resilience. I discovered that even in the darkest moments, there is strength to be found. My past taught me the value of kindness and understanding-qualities I strive to embody in my own relationships. I learnt to recognise the importance of freedom, not just for myself but for others. Everyone deserves the space to grow, to make mistakes, and to find their way without fear of judgement or retribution.

I also learnt the power of confronting the past. Unspoken truths fester, but sharing them, even years later, can bring healing. My conversation with Loren was a turning point, a reminder that I am not defined by what happened to me but by how I choose to move forward.

CHAPTER 8:
BREAKING FREE FROM THE CHAINS OF HER CONTROL

PROLOGUE

M. Scott Peck, in The Road Less Travelled, observed that 'love is the will to extend one's self for the purpose of nurturing one's own or another's spiritual growth.' But for some, love becomes a weapon, used to control and diminish.

- M. Scott Peck, The Road Less Travelled

From the moment I left her house, our relationship began to change. It might have been the distance, the fact that I was no longer under her roof or her rules. Or maybe it was because I had entered adulthood, not just as a woman but as a mother. I was no longer the child she could scold into submission, though her words still carried an invisible weight.

We lived close enough for convenience but far enough for breathing room. Despite the space, we spoke every day on the phone-short conversations about trivial things. She would complain about her job, moan about family, or dissect the latest drama in the soaps we both watched. On weekends, my daughter and I would stay over. Those visits were filled with her constant instructions-"Do not do this, "Do not touch that-but they were manageable in small doses. Knowing I would leave soon to return to my own home gave me the patience I needed.

Still, her presence was a tapestry woven with tension. Her toxic traits lingered, seeping into the cracks of our newfound dynamic. I recall one particular incident vividly. I had asked her to babysit, a favour I rarely requested. Instead of a simple answer, I was met with a lecture: "I have raised my children. They are grown. This is my time to live. Frustrated but resigned, I turned to my Aunt Cynthia, who agreed without hesitation. She even offered to collect my daughter the night before.

When that woman discovered my plan, her reaction was baffling. She demanded I retrieve my daughter from Aunt Cynthia immediately. Her tone left no room for negotiation, and though I was a grown woman, I obeyed. Years later, I learnt the full extent of her betrayal. During a time when she had fallen out with my Aunt Cynthia (fallouts with her siblings were a regular occurrence), my aunt revealed that that woman had lied, telling her that it was I that insisted my daughter be returned. The sting of that lie still burns, a betrayal wrapped in manipulation.

In my mid-twenties, I met my first husband. He was a calming presence in my often-turbulent life. But that woman despised him, and I never truly understood why. Perhaps she saw him as a rival for my attention, a threat to the control she wielded. As our relationship deepened, so did her resentment.

We married within a year and welcomed a daughter a year later. Her feelings toward him only worsened. She refused to let him cross her threshold, not once in seven years. Yet when we divorced, her attitude changed entirely. Suddenly, he was an ally, someone to commiserate with over my perceived failings. She even stood as his character witness in court when I sought custody arrangements. It was not just betrayal-it was an active celebration of my pain.

Looking back, I can see her behaviour clearly for what it was-jealousy. It was a bitter pill to swallow. Mothers are not meant to envy their daughters. They are supposed to nurture, to uplift. Yet she seemed to thrive on my struggles, basking in the glow of my failures.

The older I grew, the more I recognised her reflection in myself. Her negativity seeped into my thoughts; her argumentative nature echoed in my words. I had to confront an uncomfortable truth: I was becoming like her. It was a turning point, a moment of reckoning. I made a conscious decision to change.

Her traits were like shadows, following me even when I tried to escape them:

Every conversation revolved around her-her grievances, her triumphs, her life.

She seemed happiest when others were struggling, as if misery were a balm for her soul.

She held grudges with a fervour that was both exhausting and relentless.

Gossip was her currency, and no one was immune from her sharp tongue.

She often reduced people to stereotypes, bringing up the colour of their skin in contexts where it had no place.

Her disdain for mixed relationships was a hypocrisy I could never reconcile. Despite having siblings in such relationships, she seemed determined to impose her prejudices on me.

One memory still cuts deep. She removed photos of my daughter who is mixed-race, when work colleagues visited, as though she were something to be hidden. My children were not allowed to call her "Nan. Instead, they were instructed to address her by her name in public, an arbitrary rule that underscored her obsession with appearances.

Even her age was a fabrication. She reduced it at will, shaving years off her life to appear younger. The consequence? It made me inexplicably younger too, to the point where her fantasy would have had me giving birth as a child myself.

Emotional Reflections

I often wonder what drove her to behave as she did. Was it pain? Fear? A desperate need for control? Whatever the root, her actions shaped me in ways I am only beginning to unravel.

Her toxicity was a storm, but it taught me resilience. It taught me what kind of parent I did not want to be. It forced me to examine myself with brutal honesty, to confront the traits I had inherited, and actively choose a different path.

Lessons Learnt

From her, I learnt that blood ties are not always kind. Sometimes they are used as a weapon, wielded with precision to control and manipulate. But I also learnt that I have the power to break the cycle.

I am not her. I carry pieces of her, yes, but I have shaped them into something new-something better. The journey has been painful, filled with betrayal and heartbreak, but it has also been transformative.

That woman may never change. But I knew I had to change, and I have, and for that, I am grateful.

CHAPTER 9:
VENOM IN THE FAMILY

PROLOGUE

Gabor Maté, in When the Body Says No, writes that 'unresolved trauma is often passed down like a curse, passed from one generation to the next until someone has the courage to break the chain.' The courage to break free can be the hardest journey.

- Gabor Maté, When the Body Says No

It was either 2004 or 2005, though the exact year blurs in my memory. What remains vivid is the storm that brewed between me and that woman-a term I now find fitting, given the wedge she drove into my life. She lived next door to my childminder, and what began as minor irritations soon became an unbearable strain.

Time and again, I asked her to simply let me know when she collected my daughter so I did not have to rush home and could do things like stop off and do some shopping. It seemed such a small request-a courtesy to ease the stress of my already hectic days. Yet, she never complied.

At the time, my partner of eight months remained blissfully unaware of the tension. He had been welcomed into the family with open arms by her! She actually liked him. Had she mellowed with age? That illusion shattered the day he went to collect my daughter. She was not at the childminder's, so he knocked on that woman's door.

He made the fatal mistake of saying, "Could you let me know if and when you collect her? It was a reasonable request, but to her, it was an unforgivable affront. She erupted, her words slicing through the air with venomous precision. Her cousin stood by, silent but complicit, as my daughter witnessed the tirade. My partner was left stunned. When he got home, he tried to call her to diffuse the situation, but the abuse only escalated.

What followed were months of vile, toxic text messages. I made the mistake of engaging at first, carefully responding to each point with diplomacy. But her venom seeped through every word, and the futility of it all became clear. The messages continued even after I stopped replying-a torrent I could not block because, at the time, such technology did not exist.

When her messages stopped coming to me, they started going to my eldest daughter. She was only twelve or thirteen at the time, too young to be dragged into this mess. The messages were cruel and relentless. In the end, we had no choice but to change her phone number. The guilt I felt for exposing her to that toxicity still lingers in the back of my mind.

In the six months that followed, life moved on, though the scars remained. I threw myself into wedding preparations, determined to create a day filled with love and joy, a sanctuary from the chaos that had taken root in my life. Out of courtesy, I sent that woman an invitation. She never responded, and of course, she did not attend. History repeated itself. My second wedding where she was absent. Her only daughter getting married, her only child to marry and she was not there.

Returning from the honeymoon, my spirits were high. But there they were - two brown envelopes on the doormat, each bearing the familiar scrawl of her handwriting. One was addressed to my husband, the other to me. Except mine bore my previous married name. She knew full well I had reverted to my maiden name eighteen months prior, so this was no innocent mistake. It was a deliberate jab.

I tucked the envelopes away, not wanting to spoil the remnants of my honeymoon glow. When I finally opened them, I was in shock. Her letter to my husband was a four-page diatribe of handwritten venom. She accused him of interfering in matters concerning her granddaughter (the first and only time she used that word) and went on a tirade of character assassination. She ended with an accusation of infidelity, meticulously detailing a supposed affair on Valentine's Day. The irony of her choice of date would have been laughable if it were not so cruel.

I remember Valentine's Day that year with perfect clarity. Both my husband and I worked in Birmingham city centre. We caught the bus to work together, as always. I had taken the afternoon off to prepare a surprise for him. There was no opportunity for her story to hold even a shred of truth. But it was not the accusation that stung the most-it was the malice behind it.

The letter addressed to me was identical, word for word. It was not photocopied but painstakingly handwritten again, as if to ensure I could feel the full force of her hatred. Also inside my envelope was the wedding invitation I had sent her-ripped into pieces.

Emotional Reflections

There are moments that leave a lasting impact, and that time with her was one of them. What began as a simple request-asking her to let me know when she collected my daughter-escalated into something far darker. Her refusal to show even the smallest courtesy set the stage for months of cruelty. The constant barrage of venomous messages, especially when my daughter was dragged into it, left me exhausted and hurt.

Life moved on, but the scars remained. My wedding, a day that should have been filled with joy, was overshadowed by the letters received upon my return from our honeymoon. Letters filled with lies and venom were the final blow, but they also revealed the depth of her hatred.

Through it all, I've learnt resilience. Though the pain lingers, I now know the importance of not letting others define my worth. Some storms break you, but they also help you rebuild.

Lessons Learnt

Looking back, I can see how her actions shaped my resilience. At the time, I felt powerless, overwhelmed by the weight of her malice. But in the chaos, I learnt to protect my peace. I learnt to walk away from battles that could not be won and to place boundaries around my heart and my family.

That woman's behaviour was not about me or my husband. It was a reflection of her own turmoil-a storm she refused to confront within herself. While her words cut deep, they also taught me the importance of breaking cycles of toxicity, especially for the sake of my daughters.

I have chosen to forgive her-not for her sake, but for mine. Forgiveness does not mean forgetting, nor does it mean allowing her back into my life. It means releasing the hold her actions had over me. It means choosing love over bitterness and peace over chaos.

These moments, as painful as they were, became a testament to my strength. They reminded me that even in the darkest chapters, we hold the power to turn the page and write a new story.

CHAPTER 10:
GASLIGHTING AND GRUDGES: THE NARCISSIST'S PLAYBOOK

PROLOGUE

Narcissistic people can be incredibly toxic. They believe that the world revolves around them, and when you do not play by their rules, they will do everything in their power to punish you.

- Lundy Bancroft, Why Does He Do That?

When my second daughter was born, my eldest was only seven. For reasons I do not fully understand, she chose to confide in her grandmother, telling her that my husband was being cruel to her, verbally abusive. Yet, instead of taking action, instead of listening or coming to me or confronting my husband directly-actions I would expect from anyone, especially a professional-she dismissed my daughter's plea for intervention, telling her, "Don't be silly."

Can you believe that woman my daughter's grandmother who had a duty of care to ensure her safety and emotional well-being? Instead of providing the protection my daughter so desperately needed, she failed her in a way that remains incomprehensible to me.

Not only that, instead of seeking support from her peers or professionals to offload her own stresses, she burdened my eldest daughter-who was just a child herself-with both her personal and work-related problems. My daughter, already facing the challenges of being a preteen, had to bear the weight of an adult's emotional turmoil without the understanding or support she needed.

It wasn't until my daughter was an adult that she opened up to me about the burdens she had shouldered. Only then did I learn how deeply this emotional neglect had affected her while she was growing up. What angers me most is the terrifying thought of what could have happened had my now ex-husband's behaviour escalated to physical abuse. The truth remains, though, that both my daughter and I were failed in the most fundamental way by the one person who should have been her protector.

Unlike the woman, who had no qualms about dissing me to others in front of and even directly to my children-who were around five and twelve at the time-I chose not to poison their minds against her. The fallout was between me and that woman, not her and my children. I allowed them to visit her, believing that despite everything, they deserved to have their own relationship with her.

However, that belief was tested when I learnt about the conversations she was having with or in front of my children. The things she said were unacceptable and I made the decision to stop their visits for a while. When I eventually reinstated them, my eldest daughter, by then old enough to understand the dynamics, decided she no longer wanted to visit her nan, aka Mrs. Brown, anymore. It was her decision, and as her mother, I had to respect it.

From that point on, that woman's behaviour took a more deliberate and cruel turn. Whenever she saw both of my daughters out and about, she would speak to my youngest and completely ignore my eldest, as if she did not exist. It was not a one-off occurrence. It happened time and again, each instance driving the wedge deeper.

One particular incident remains etched in my memory. My eldest was with a friend who had come to visit from out of town. They were out together when they crossed paths with that woman-her nan, aka Mrs. Brown, though she insisted on being called Mrs. Brown. My eldest, ever the respectful child I raised her to be, greeted her grandmother, with a polite hello. Despite the effort my daughter made to be courteous, that woman's response was chilling. She looked her directly in the eyes and then turned away without a word, as though she were invisible. My eldest, resilient and brave, chose to rise above it, but the scars of those encounters are ones I will never forget.

How could a grown woman treat a child, her own grandchild, with such calculated cruelty?

The woman was not content with turning my extended family against me, leaving me with only my daughters, my brother, and my father. She then set her sights on driving a wedge between me and my brother. Imagine a woman who never shows emotion or sheds a tear suddenly calling my brother in tears, blaming my husband for everything that had been happening. My brother, who had never seen this side of her, must have thought she was genuinely affected, and this influenced him to call my house, threatening my husband.

When that did not achieve the desired result, she escalated her tactics. She called my brother and told him she was sending him a text message-not to read it, but simply to copy, paste, and send it to me. When my brother relayed this to me, he said, "If I had sent the message to you, you would never have spoken to me again. To this day, I still do not know what the contents of that message were, but I know she had crafted it as though it had come from him, directed at me. That, to me, is the very definition of narcissistic, toxic behaviour.

Despite all of her efforts, my bond with my brother remained intact. So much so that when my Aunt Cynthia passed away, the woman instructed him not to share the funeral details with me, hoping to prevent me from attending. He disregarded her demands, and I attended the funeral. It was the first time I had seen my extended family since the fallout. Some members completely ignored me, while others spoke to me only reluctantly, making an already painful day even more difficult.

Emotional Reflection

The betrayal still lingers. My daughter, just seven years old, sought protection from her grandmother but was met with cruel dismissal. Instead of support, she was burdened with adult problems and left to navigate emotional neglect on her own. The calculated rejection my child endured is incomprehensible and remains a painful reminder of how trust can be shattered by those meant to protect.

Lessons Learnt

This experience taught me the importance of listening to children and valuing their voices. It also reinforced the need to set firm boundaries with toxic individuals, no matter their role in the family. Above all, I have learned that resilience and healing come from prioritising love, respect, and protection over toxic ties.

CHAPTER 11:

CUTTING TIES, RECLAIMING PEACE

PROLOGUE

The greatest tragedy of life is not what we suffer, but what we allow to continue when we have the power to change it.

- Robin Sharma

After the fallout, the woman made it her mission to badmouth me to anyone who would listen. She spun her version of events to anyone who would lend an ear-family, friends, and likely even the postman. This had a devastating impact on my relationship with my extended family, which was the hardest part to bear, as I had been very close to them. In time, though, it became more bearable. She also ensured our mutual hairdresser was involved, and after hearing her side, decided I was at fault; I was left with no option but to find a new one.

The constant refrain of "She is your mother, "You cannot fall out with your mother, and "You need to make up with her became tiresome. People seemed to forget that no one truly understood what I had been through-they only heard her perspective. In any situation, there are always three sides to every story: yours, theirs, and the truth.

I opened up to a few close friends, sharing everything I had endured since the fallout. As I revealed more, their understanding deepened, and they came to respect my decision to cut that woman out of my life.

Narcissists thrive on your reactions. The satisfaction they get from knowing their actions or words affect you is their source of gratification. When they do not get the reaction they want, they will find new ways to provoke you. This was evident when she sided with my first husband after our divorce-it never bothered me; to be honest, I found it quite amusing. Two people who have disliked each other for years are forming an alliance. However, four years ago, when my youngest daughter found out she was pregnant, she chose to confide in her nan, aka Mrs. Brown, first, rather than me or her dad. The response she received mirrored exactly what I went through twenty-nine years earlier: she was told she was a disgrace to the family and urged to get rid of the baby. It was a perfect example of history repeating itself.

What made it even more hypocritical was the fact that this woman had a child (me) after being involved with a married man; whether she knew he was married at the time is unclear. Aged nineteen, unemployed with no career. This is coming from a woman who judged my daughter, who was 22, in a committed relationship, with a law degree and a bright future ahead of her.

Around 2008, I received news from my brother that she was in the hospital due to heart problems. It made me think that life was too short to hold onto the past, so I decided to try and put it behind us. Though I hadn't forgiven her or forgotten what had happened, our relationship had changed. We weren't close, but we were talking again. I would stop by her house-I still lived just around the corner-but it was always for some sort of favour, not for socialising.

This brief period of peace, however, was short-lived. Her toxic nature soon resurfaced. It was around the time my cousin got married that I made the decision to let my youngest daughter go with that woman to the wedding in London. I could not afford to take all four of us, as it would require travel and accommodation costs. But when my daughter returned promptly after they returned, missing me, it was not seen as an innocent wish to come home. Instead, she blamed me, accusing me of somehow making my daughter want to leave. That was the moment I realised that she would never change. It was time to cut her out of my life for good.

To sever ties with toxic people, it is essential to clearly and firmly communicate your decision to distance yourself. Establish strong boundaries and limit or cease contact where necessary. Blocking them on communication platforms can provide additional protection. Prioritise your well-being by seeking support from trusted friends or family, and if the situation feels overwhelming, consider seeking professional guidance from a therapist.

In my own experience, I took drastic measures to protect myself. I cut contact, changed my phone number, moved house, and limited my conversations about what I was going through with a few close friends since my family had sided with that woman. Although I did not seek professional help at the time, I now realise it might have been a valuable step.

Between 2013 and 2017, I took two actions as part of my healing process:

I left a voicemail for the woman, saying, "I forgive you.

I sent an email to all my aunts and uncles. I began by clarifying that this message was not to criticise their sister or recount my side of the story. Thinking as I composed it, that if they had cared and wanted to hear my side of the story, they would have reached out at the time. I did not expect them to care now. Instead, I reminded them of the numerous arguments and fallouts each of them had experienced with her, highlighting the recurring common denominator. My goal was to give them food for thought and perhaps lead them to question the version of events they had accepted.

And in those moments of drastic action, I unknowingly took the first steps toward reclaiming my peace and beginning the journey of healing.

Bumping into her was inevitable, given that we lived so close. I had grown accustomed to her avoiding gaze-preferring to face a brick wall as we passed to avoid the risk of eye contact. We walked past each other as if we were strangers.

Recently, we found ourselves at the local gym at the same time. Despite five vacant exercise bikes, she chose the one right next to me. Why? The question raced through my mind. In the past, I would have gotten up and moved, but not anymore. I completed my workout; her presence no longer affected me.

Emotional Reflections

Letting go of someone who should have been a cornerstone of my life was agonising. The fallout with her was not just a loss of relationship but a loss of trust and belonging. The web of manipulation and lies she spun left me alienated from my extended family, people I had once cherished deeply. Her smear campaign was not merely a personal attack; it felt like a public trial where the verdict had been decided without my testimony. The pain of having my truth dismissed by those I held dear left scars that I carry to this day. Yet, amidst the pain, I found clarity-I realised that holding on to a toxic connection was far more damaging than the heartbreak of letting go.

Lessons Learnt

I learned that protecting your peace is an act of courage. Establishing boundaries is not selfish; it is necessary. Narcissists may try to control the narrative, but their power diminishes when you refuse to engage. Reaching out to my aunts and uncles was not an attempt to change their minds but an effort to reclaim my voice. It taught me the value of speaking up for myself, even when others refuse to listen. Forgiving her was not about her-it was about freeing myself. Healing begins when you let go of the need for closure from someone incapable of giving it and instead find it within yourself.

CHAPTER 12:
A FLICKER OF HOPE

PROLOGUE

Maya Angelou once said that in the face of adversity, the human spirit has an incredible ability to endure, to overcome, and to thrive. It is in the most difficult of times that we truly understand our potential, for strength is not born in moments of ease, but in the fire of trials and tribulations. Through these challenges, we are not only tested, but forged into the people we are meant to be.

- Maya Angelou

As I journey through life, I know it is inevitable that I will encounter moments that test my strength. At times, it feels as though I am lost in the dark, searching for a way forward with no end in sight. But I have come to realise-within me, there is always a flicker of light. It is a quiet, unwavering presence, one that holds the power to guide me through even the most uncertain of times. This spark, this hope, is what carries me through the hardest days and leads me towards a strength I might not even know I possess.

The road to healing is rarely a smooth one. It winds and turns, often without warning, taking me to places I never expected to go. But in every twist, every step, there is an opportunity for growth. Every small victory, every moment of courage, no matter how seemingly insignificant, is a victory nonetheless. And with each step, I come closer to the peace and strength I seek. So, even when the path seems long or the weight too heavy, I keep moving forward. I am not defined by how quickly I reach my destination but by my resilience in the face of the journey.

Resilience is not about never falling. It is about the courage to rise again and again, each time with a heart that is wiser and stronger than before. I will stumble, as we all do, but it is in those moments of vulnerability that I discover the true depth of my strength. It is not about avoiding hardship; it is about choosing to face it head-on, with grace, with determination, and with the knowledge that I am capable of more than I realise. And in those moments, I remind myself that every setback, every obstacle, is simply another step in my journey to becoming the person I am meant to be. My strength lies not just in overcoming the challenges but in embracing them as part of the path that leads me to my fullest self.

And when the weight of the world feels unbearable, I remind myself: hope is a choice. It is a choice to believe that I am worthy of all the joy, growth, and love that life has to offer. It is a choice to see the possibility in every moment, even when the future seems uncertain. I have everything within me to overcome whatever challenge stands before me, and there is nothing I cannot endure. I know now that my inner strength is limitless, and each challenge I face is shaping me into someone capable of creating the life I desire. I am not just surviving-I am thriving, becoming more resilient with every step.

No matter how fierce the storm may seem, I know that it will pass. The skies will clear, the sun will shine, and I will emerge stronger than before. I hold onto that hope. I trust in myself and my journey. And I always remember, I am never alone. Even in the most solitary moments, there is a connection to something greater, something that will carry me through to brighter days. In those darkest times, I have learnt that even the smallest glimmer of hope can be enough to spark the strength I need to move forward. So, I hold my head high and keep moving forward, knowing that my journey is one of strength, resilience, and ultimately, hope-a hope that will never fade as long as I continue to believe in myself. And I carry this truth with me: I am not just surviving this moment; I am transforming, evolving, and stepping into a future that is filled with endless possibilities.

Your thoughts matter.

If *Raised by a Narcissist: That Woman aka My Mother* spoke to you, I would be deeply grateful if you would take a moment to leave a review.

Please return to the place where you bought or listened to your copy, whether that was Amazon, Audible, Goodreads, Barnes & Noble, Waterstones, Spotify or another trusted bookseller and share your thoughts.

Your feedback helps other readers discover stories that resonate, and it supports authors like me in continuing to share work that matters.

Thank you for reading and for being part of this journey.

Serena Bennett

Printed in Dunstable, United Kingdom

80721353R00060